Simon +
Kim,
love,
Fiona

THE UNIVERSE AND ME
TORIA GARBUTT

The Universe and Me
Toria Garbutt

ISBN 978-1-903110-60-7
First published in this edition 2018 by Wrecking Ball Press.

Cover design by humandesign.co.uk

LOTTERY FUNDED · ARTS COUNCIL ENGLAND
Supported using public funding by

CONTENT

SUBWAY

That inbetween space
in Ferry shop square
where girls and boys
can
kick spit kick bins
sweat
shiver and swear
gob off at coppers
spray words on t'wall
like BAZ 4 SHAZ
TLFE
or
I WOZ ERE
IDST
just hangin around
drinkin Twenny Twenny
Yeah mate
I WOZ ERE
for some reason
I never understood
raight ere in Knottla
instead of Hollywood in 1933
nah, not me mate,
I woz ere
Knottla
1993
where
Tracey's got AIDS
and SHAZ IS A SLAG

and TWOKKOS A PUFF
and TINA'S ON SKAG
and PACKIS DUNT FUCKIN BELONG OWWER ERE
yeh that's where I wa mate
I WOZ ERE
"I've driven through it" everyone goes
that inbetween place
that nobody knows
where nobody's bin
n nobody's stopped
incase their fuckin wheeltrims
get ripped off
nobody's has a sarnie on Racca Green
nobody's stopped at Morag's
for a pot of hot tea
nobodys nipped through t'snicket
at t'back o GTs
where t'words are still on t'wall
from 1984
THATCHER FUCKED US UP

I WANNA BE ADORED

and nothing feels better than this
sweat sticks hair
to heads
and lips
to lips
and each molecule of you
is incredible
I just can't fucking
believe it
you're a miracle
it's might be chemically induced
but it's still true
I just cunt normally
say it
I fucking love you

I can feel
the bass
in my belly
all t' way through
I want to peel your top off
and get on top of you
roll around
in oceans of feathers
make this moment
last forever
wings are growing
from shoulders
like ethers

we are all god
and this is our heaven

FORGIVE

I dint wanna be a mam
it want
in any way
a part of my plan
dint gush and coo
owwer baby grows
in Mothecare
or silver cross prams

Dint care for soft towels and
sweet pink skin
not me
on t' top floor of a block o flats
in Ferry
I dreamed of better things

Of packing my bags and leaving him
of flying high and
making marks
not finger shaped
and blue
like t' ones
wrapped round my arms
but big ones
bold and beautiful

But it was
too late
for this mistake

Bed made
Price paid
I stayed

Smiled through denial
folded
babygrows
into neat piles
made checklists
stayed stick thin
convinced missen
that destiny
had sent me
to save him

And you grew
upside down
breach
got cut out
and extracted
by blue plastic fingers

They wrapped you up
like a glow worm
and let me
take pictures

That first night
I sin ya

beady eyed
like a ninja
convinced
that care order
mam
opposite
wa coming
to pinch you
my heart
like a drill
in my chest
restless
and soaked in sweat
and these women
in white who
said they knew best
were a threat

And in the early hours
the apple on my tray
became a baby's head
severed and mocking
and wanting you dead
I cried all the next day
and the midwife
said
it was textbook
day two
baby blues

and asked if I'd
breast fed

Regret begot regret
and I dropped you
on concrete
You fell
four feet
face first
in your first week
and that was all
the proof I needed
of my inadequacy
this motherhood
a fallacy

I hid bottles
from the midwife
ashamed
let you suck
on empty nipples
in this game we were playing
I was the enemy
cheated the tests
so nobody'd
take ya
battled dark desires
that begged me to shake ya
then sobbed with shame

while I left you to cry
frantic all croaky throat wondering why
noone was coming
to sooth you
Instead I trained you
restrained you
sometimes felt
like I hated you

Resented deeply
my loss of freedom
see I was a slave
in his majesty's kingdom
and life was restricted
diluted
a series of pictures
presented in intricate
porcelain stitches
I resisted the urge
to pull
and pick

Bashed my head
instead
cut my legs in t' bath
and watched
as thin ribbons danced
around my arms
cool and calm

Shit mum!
Ugly Cunt !
his words
scarred
and I,
fucked up,
held him harder

Prayed and prayed and prayed and prayed
gi missen away
like bait
tried to please
and attracted
instead
more hate
too late
to leave
too late
too late
one more on the way

I laid
a fresh new chick
in softer hay
soothed some of
my darkest thoughts
away
made best

of the mess
began to accept
noone is perfect
reflect

Dared to dream again and
asked the universe for alignment
burned Gina Ford and read instead
Dayna Martin
broke out of the
illusion
of solitary confinement

and at last
after a decade
I packed
ran from the hills
never looked back
took the boys
to the city
and built my own nest
grew new wings
to protect
new words
that sounded like
self respect
friends who stuck around
despite my absence

poets who were willing
to give me chances
pens
with which
to write
new chapters
and the knowledge
there is always
always hope

in my darkest hours
when I lost the skills
to cope
when I struggled
to find the flowers
she said
know
that I've been there too
and the most important
thing you must remember
to do
is your best
sometimes that might be
accepting
you're depressed
allowing yourself
to stay in bed
undressed

letting yourself heal, rest
sister
we are all
perfectly imperfect

Be kind
to yourself and
just keep breathing
never ever stop believing
visualise
and manifest
we're the winners
out of 250 million sperm cells
we've already passed the test

Lets live every second like our last
keep the past where it belongs, in the past
wrap up our bairnes and keep em close
cherish the ones we love the most
let guilt be free like fire flies
it's the only way to live
rise high like enchanted lanterns
and forgive yourself , my love
forgive

FIRST KISS

My first ever kiss
wa John Paul Kowalczyk
K-O-W-A-L-C-Z-Y-K
his mam wa called Julie
and his granddad wa Polish
and a know this
cos ad loved him
for years
held his hand
in mi head
 hundreds o times
hoped n hoped
one day
he'd be mine
but I want cool
not one bit
an then in year six
I got fit
n he asked me art
wow man
a cunt believe it
IT girls swarmed around
like bees
socked pulled up
raight owwer t'knees
'Johnpaul sez will you meet him?'
Me wi my boyfriend
n them wi theirs
six of us

lined up in pairs
against t'concrete wall
o t'sports centre
necking
We necked loads
after that
in ginnels
darn snickets
up park
darn t'Quack
you coggied me
up Broomhill n back
mi knight in shining
shellsuit
d'ya remember that time on mi bed?
you tasted like chicken tikka
your tongue wa
proper freezin
you wa eager
you went
'let's kiss like they do it on t'tele'
squished your lips all owwer mine
n all t'time
am feelin sorry for t'chicken
thinkin how your breath
wa stinkin of spices
n flesh
I brushed mi teeth
as soon as you left

You gi mi glass for gifts
we lit incense sticks
n listened
 to Gabrielle
we smoked together as well
JP N VIKKI
TLFE
true love forever
IDST
our love wa boundless
it grew n grew n grew
n then on t'day before highschool
I dumped you

BETTER LEFT ALONE

Sometimes am better left alone
to cry n that
when t'fizz o t'champagne's
gone flat
and laughter's laughed its fuckin head off
when av ad enough
just leave me alone fed up n owwer fed n wrapped up
leave me tucked up in mi blue cocoon
leave me watching
1950s subtitled black n white cartoons
When it's all become too much at once to even try
I'm better let to DIY
to cry n hurl all t'pain art
n once it's art it's art
n I'm empty n floating n there's nowt left to cry abart
When guilt pulls mi stomach through mi throat
like a plunger
and mi limbs have turned to sandbags and they're dragging me under
I'm better left alone to count t'gaps between t'thunder
n stay inside mi quilt until t'storm's blown owwer
Til it's breezy and hollow in mi blue cocoon
and I'm rising
and I'm rising
like a helium balloon
and I've licked all t'sticky syrup off t'medicine spoon
n I've howled missen hoarse to a hot plastic moon

NOWT MATTERS NOW

In Knottla
we smoke smack
for pain
to hide the guilt
and blame
and shame
of unemployment
We play guitars
and gaze at stars
to feel warm
and safe
and happy
We're grungers
and flower children
90s mop haired lovers
and swaggers
who pile into
transit vans
and blag it
into Glastonbury
Our art is beautiful
it's Hendrix n Pixies
n 60s psychedelia
n Cecelia is brekkin
are hearts man
she's brekkin are
fuckin hearts
Oasis hats
tinnies n flares

Britpop blasts n blares
through Warwick Estate
on carnival day
we win goldfish
then we eat em
for dares
Act a twat
infront o t'mayor o Ponte
'are kid' this n 'are kid' that
are nasal tones raight
suited Manc
mi mate Roachy
wa mad for it man
He showed me this trick
wi his fist
in t'pissin darn rain
in t'park
we held invisible umbrellas
owwer us heads
n stayed art til dark
dry as mi nanna's scones mate
You wa this ballerina boy
in a hat
on a mission to Brov woods
wi a guitar on your back
wi weed n beer n stories
n smack
n all t'time in t'world
to do mad stuff like that

Thought we'd be here forever
weightless n old
burnin rocks
instead of coal
burnin for us fathers
n us grand father's souls
But muckers dunt stay muckers
when t'sun's gone down
when t'honeymoon is owwer
n you're rattlin for t'brown
n you'd rob your mother's
wedding ring
n flog it up town
cos nothing is sacred
when t'sun's gone down
When you're gagging
for a bag
n your nose is on t'drip
n you'd tek your mam's
last tenner
for a quick n easy fix
cos nowt matters nar mucker
nowt matters nar
That night you walked home
from your dad's
you dint mek it
past t'railway tracks
wa you actin stupid?
Did you lay down to look at stars

n fall asleep?
Or did you weep
n wait for death
to tek you?
Mate
I wish that I'd bin with you
cos id've held mi fist above you
n kept you dry

LETTER TO MY SISTER

I'm writing you this while you're still alive
I say these words wiart really letting em inside
cause if I do they'll kill me
n wi all t'wll in t'world
I can't detach from t'pain
of never seeing my big sister again
and I'm frightened
I dunt wanna be at your funeral
head hung low
stomach thick wi sick
n sorrow
mouth agape in disbelief
and wish a coulda told you this
so here it is
An, you're fucking beautiful
rooted in good soil
you stand tall like a sunflower
and dance
A crack house is no castle for a Princess, An
no way they can see you sparkle in t'dark
a lighter is no spotlight for a star
Dya remember how we useda imagine
another world beneath t'quilt
where we lay
perfectly still n magicked chocolate
how you played upside down chords
on t'guitar
bizarre
the way that you did that

that lass that you brayed on my behalf
Thankyou for being my sister
for the Doors and Nirvana and black eyeliner
for the times I've cried and you've made it better
n yeah there's been shit ones too
I'm sorry for the hurt I've caused you
that I can't be with you now
it dunt mean I dunt love ya
you're my sister
and you're close to my heart
too fucking close
and you're the master of tearing it apart
and it's fragile
I wish you well
I believe you can get clean
that connection is the cure to your disease
that you can heal
and spread your wings
and be free

BEACH

you lose I heard someone say
and then the flames lickin their limbs
wi its quick wet tongue
spittin fast new feelings n mi mouth's
beginning to bleed like metal
dry art like gravel
rolled art from t'sea
n am starting to see man
a think yeah man
real eyes realise real lies man
this feels right man
this feels right
and t'smell of his coat from mi grandma's attic
easy and free
n rollin it on t'sea breaze
a thin flirtatious wisp
n my hair on his chest
crisp like seaweed
sucked art moisture
like spiders' feet
teardrops cuttin through deepest sleep
and darkest skin
n his mam's voice beneath the sand
and sounds sit crucified
and yeah man
do we empathise
n someone beside me is
stickin skins
a can't feel em

he says
cos they feel too thin
n they feel like nowt
n mi head'll explode
n tiny shards might scatter
we're all the same
he said he said
all of us
he said he said
just molecules
he said he said
we're all the same
he said
this sand
he said
these shells
he said
just cells
he said he said he said
we're all the same
he said he said
all the same he said
I saw what he saw
n I said what he said
cause all I ever wanted to do wa dance wi the boys the lights
creating this cosmic display like paint blown through a straw
on t'second day o school and Mrs Spears wi her pinny tied in
a bow at the back and his breath like coffee as he leaned over
he said a word after school wa all he wa after and then Lindsy

read the horoscopes and finished off the voddy and then we
went to school and we dint tell anybody that I wa gettin pissed
and she wa getting laid and he wa teachin music and gettin
fuckin paid and then
we're back on t'beach again laughing and bouncing like feral
clowns
until somebody screamed
n there wa nowt but silence
nowt except the fire hissing and screeching and Joplin calling
out for her Bobby Mcgee through haunted faces and now the
dance is demonic the dance is demonic and it dunt feel safe
anymore and I'm losing it
this way that way this way
What?
Did somebody just say summat?
What?
Did somebody just say summat?
it's just cause I thought that you wa talking forwards and I wa
talking backwards and I thought we might just meet up in
t'middle or summat
did I say that out loud?
in t'middle or summat
did I say it out loud?
this way that way this way that way
down down down into cold sweat and feverish panic
and mi eyes are trying to focus on these
secrets puzzles secrets puzzles
and I can't even
secrets puzzles secrets puzzles

until somebody says
shhhhhhhhhhhhh
it's ok it's ok everything's ok
and like limestone to water
and Calpol to fever
I'm clear

TWO LITTLE DUCKS

She collects feathers and receipts each time they meet
cause in times of depression and retreat
they bring comfort
His green souvenir pen lends solace
to a stormy morning when t'thought
of getting out of bed
kicks her in t'stomach
and flips t'off switch in her head
A text from him can force her downstairs
to light incense and make coffee instead
stand in a hinata in t'kitchen
n try to think of happy things
wear that mustard woolly cardie
that stinks of festivals and him
and innit mad how she forgets
how deep and dark the pain can get
how worry can make her immobile
She hoards thoughts and memories
like a magpie
eagle eyed for romantic detail
and a heart that's full to bursting
and it does
it deflates her
she has these intense moments
of doubt
where she hates her
and the onny way she can think to escape her
is bed
a white synthetic pillow

pressed to her head
and the lights off
and when it stops
his feather can be a magic wand
that drifts
fits lightly in fingertips
flips switches and lifts
a gift
Time goes fast when they meet
they spend impossible hours
dancing on t'beach
til t'tide rolls in
and forces defeat
she writes
two little ducks
in t'sand wi her feet
and they scarper

YELLOW SPELL LAUGHTER

and the yellow spell laughter
came back
to delight and dance
and calm the tacky glare
of adolescence
and smooth the cracks
that vanity made
and the words came tumbling back
one
at
a
time
onto t'page
Hard handed cartwheels
watching grass breathe
crawling round t'city
on us hands n knees
are mucky
eyes are wide
and there's this feeling
in mi stomach
like it's gunna be alright
Let's drink away the Jarman blues
wi Big In Booze wine
Let's wrap up in t'bed sheets
on t'broken washing line
Let's get high like it's
1969
Let's be Janis Joplin

Let's do the bear
Let's nick eachother's straighteners
and Primark underwear
Let's eat too much Cheesecake
cocker
come on tek chance
cause the yellow spell laughter's
come back to dance

FOR HANNAH

Vibe lifter
mixer of medicinal herbs
you are naked as children
a new born babe in my world
you are freedom and soul
like Yorkshire stone
you are mermaid and beauty and earth
and home
Fixer of things
peace maker
wise at birth
beyond your years
instinctive
and the sweetest sounds rise high from your lips
carry love like mothers' hips
you are warmth and truth and trust
and bliss
and I knew you in an instant
remembered nights we whispered spells
on hilltops
forgot how much i missed you sister
til we met again
and now we can start to unpack
take off the rucksack and lay it flat
soothe chaos with oceans of calm
move mountains with strong Yorkshire arms
run fast
sup pints
and howl at moons together

BLUE ROOMS

it's been two years since we met
and I'm back in t'Blue Rooms
supping strong Jamaican stout
writing about how waiting for you
is one of my favourite things to do
I'll buy you one when you arrive
watch you smile and get loose
turn every single head in t'room
we might even have two and a packet of crisps
and that first time we met here my parka stank of skunk
and you said "there are worse things to smell of, Garbutt"
and I'm glancing through t'window
for your shape and mop and swag
for your skinny jeans and doccers and merchandise bag
but when you arrive there's this look in your eyes
that says 'summat's up mate'
and I take on your pain like a sponge in t'rain
we sit heavy together and eat
talk abart ambition, adventures and dreams
sigh for loss of those we love
but must leave

THE UNIVERSE AND ME

That inbetween space
after school
before tea

just t' sunshine
and t' tele
and t' settee
and me

tired and happy and hollow
and free

just t'sunshine
and t' tele
and t' settee
and me

A waft o' snags n mash n that comes curlin across t'room
n mi mam's mekkin up all t'words
to a 90s britpop tune

she's like

"girls who are boys who are boys who are girls who are deee
 deee dee deee you an meeee baybeee"

aww bless her little socks off
they're soft n pink n cotton

she'lla probly a bobbly cardi on
but dunt ask cos av forgotten

she's small n cute n mumsical
a twirling ballerina
she's Andy Pandy
Bill n Ben
in our livin room arena

Mi mam mi mam
she's chopping Spam
she's feeding our Chihuahua
she's teaching me the elegance
of matriarchal power

she's spinning plates on rollerskates
n servin wi a smile
she's sat her arse on t'toilet
so she'll probly be a while

It smells of snags n peas n mash
n tastes like Bisto gravy
it feels like fur
it sounds like Blur
it's the year of Achtung, baby!

It looks like suns n moons n stars
n giant yellow teacups

it feels like docs n knee high socks
n Marks n Spencers C cups

That inbetween space
after tea
before bed
when you're meant to do your homework
but you're watching Friends instead
listenin to Jim Morrison
n floating art yer head
in a higher dimension
than Knottla

Puffin on a Lambert
on a pink blow up settee
in that inbetween space
before bed
after tea
Praying for forgiveness
Praying to be free
just t'sunset
n t'moonlight
n t'universe
n me

WE'LL DANCE TO MADONNA LIKE WE USED TO

Drugs are fucking everywhere
up noses down throats
of them who hurt the most
them who are lonely
and aching and dying to feel loved
Drugs feel good
in the absence of connection
we seek compensation
in self medication
umbilical sherbet
whisky and coke
owt to fill the hole
and be whole again
Drugs are fucking everywhere
in lungs in veins
in t'blood of those we love and hate
at once
Those who hunt for smack in daytime
top up wi tapped tenners
n methadone by twilight
or those who live the highlife
sniffing charlie in the night time
it's all the same in the end

I've lost friends and family
to the veiled imposter
cost me my sister
promised you'd look after her
dint you?

I wish you'd give her back to me
it's fucking sinister
watching you eat her alive
Drugs feel good
in the absence of connection
if I open up my arms though
will I die of suffocation?
I'm barely afloat
in my sea of realisation
n if I take you in I'll drown
before I've reached my destination
But I'll see you there sister
You'll be wild and free
floating in on t'sea breeze
you'll reach out to me
and we'll dance to Madonna
like we used to

BERNER'S STREET

We hung art in this pub
called t'Dog in Ponte
propped us skateboards up
against t'fireplace
n we skanked
to Anal Soda
Did t'Okey Cokey
on t'dancefloor
saved eachother twos
on t'bines
drank bottles o cheap wine
n White Lightening
Waddled around
in these massive
low slung
baggies
wi us arses angin art
like we'd shit ussens
Us lasses wore pigtails
n pink plastic jewellery
we wa well cool
in us Marvin Martian Tshirts
n beenies
skin adorned wi piercings
us three freaks
from Knottla
n a gang o punks
from Ponte
Pink and blue

and green
and Amber
the Queen of our castle
less hassle
in Ponte
more tolerant
o moshers
they wa so much
posher than us
it wa lovely
they dint fleg in your hair
or owt
N then you came art o t'blue
wi your band
from Wakey
your Kurt Cobain twin
n his Courtney bride
n I wa this black eyed
mop haired
Mia
n you wa mi Nancy boy
this skinny thing
in pink eye shadder
n pvc
you ad a penchant for all things
glamorous
n weed
went at it like horny rabbits
on speed

n shacked ussens up
back in Wakey
 Jazzed up us home
wi tiaras n barbies
pink fluffy feathers
n sparkly cardies
you wa mine
I wa yours
we wa blissfully barmy
rowing for kicks
like Sid n Nancy
but both of us sorta loved it
dint we?
Remember that time you puked
on t'settee?
you'd ad a bottle o voddy
for tea
you wa wilder n cooler
n thinner than me
in us little inner terrace
on Berners Street

WHAT ABOUT ME

And one day
I wa laid in the bath
in our flat
n you wa at your mam's
takin solace from the chaos
n it dawned on me
like a rat in my stomach
you wa fuckin someone else
I got a taxi to your mam's
an I sin you through t'window
laughin on t'phone
n I knew it wa her
that girl from the gig
you'd rolled her a cig
n licked it wi your lyin tongue
And then you smiled at me
your old lolly stick
you wa quick
to throw me out
'go home Vikki'
you said
I ransacked your room instead
looked under the bed
upturned a stash of
photos
promises
pet names
like 'bear bear'
doodles of hearts and cribs

'go home Vikki'
and that wa that
I packed up the flat
n the cat n that
n I rented this cottage in Ponte
wi a garden shed
n a watering can
n a porch wi a rack
for your shoes
well, not yours
cos you wa gone
to Chicago
and anyway
your winkle pickers
would av looked shit
in Ponte
I'm fine
I'm thin
I'm better off without him
I'll just waste away
for a while
like a waif
all flakey n gaunt
like a junkie rag doll
deviod of the ego
that kept me alive
back in the day
with the schtick
and the kicks

the I dunt gi a shit persona
that wa blown to bits
find a new thing
let the phone ring
dial 1471
every time it stops
go to the beach
fall in love
not really
pretend
n get your heart shit on
all over again
n go back home
n do another line
n another
n another
n another
am fine
all brazen n gutsy
n head-held-high
in the Escobar toilets
I wanted to die
the worst ever advert
for Tony n Guy
bed headed
back combed
pie eyed
grimy skin
all kite-faced

hoover-nosed
black eyed
spotty chin
I made my return
on your wedding do
and I shook her hand
fuckin desperate for you
she wa little n cute
n her name sounded hot
Olivia Arduini
what's that girl got
that I ant got?
a dunt get it dunt get it
so I got a nose job
n I stopped watching Friends
n I stayed in my bedroom
listening to The End

She wa yanky n purty
n older than you
n you dumped her
at the end of December 02
had me again
on Valentine's day
got me hooked
on oxytocin
n got your end away
n fucked off
back on tour

and on the front of NME
and then I heard your song
at number 23
and the girl on the cover
looked just like me

BIRD THAT GOT AWAY

My youngest boy
he squeaks
four words
"Rosy's killed a bird"
I arm myself
with the sweeping brush
shuffle
half looking
into the kitchen
The cat
slinks slyly into
sight slitty
wild eyes
wiser now
feather
stuck to nose
like a prize
I'm disgusted
and loveless
a hole gapes
in my stomach
the children hide
We can't look
we turn our backs
on our pet
repulsed
Then suddenly
a scratching!
Frantic tiny taps

on tiles
it lifts and hits
misses in its panic
alerts the cat
who turns back
its last chance
it gives all
flies high now
hits a wall
but dunt stop trying
til it sees light
and trees

I throw open
the window
and the bird is free

CUPS OF TEA AND ME

Sometimes there is only
cups of tea and me
and seven bourbon biscuits
and a strange smell about me
and everything you do
I hate
and everything you say
makes me cry
and I want you to hold me
pull me into your chest and say
"there there" stuff like that
and I want to hold your hand
and make you bleed a bit
only a bit
cause everything you say
I hate
and everything you do
makes me cry
and you'll say
"there there" stuff like that
"you are perfect perfect perfect perfect"
but no matter what you say
I'll cry anyway
I am hopeless and insane

LITTLE FLAT IN FERRY

We lived on t'top floor of a block o flats
on Argyle Road in Ferry
dint pay us taxes or utility bills
sprayed silver paint
on t;windowcills
drew rainbows on t'walls wi chalk
wrapped up warm for flyagaric walks
round Fairburn Ings
drove back
still wildly tripping
talked abart 'terrible worms'
n pissed ussens laughing
grew a sea o green in t'attic
mate!
You wa fantastic at it
ad never sin owt like it in mi life
I wa mallory knox in us tower block
your long haired
black eyed
gypsy bride
there wa never any need to go artside
we had everything we ever needed
squeezed every inch of eachother's flesh

tangled up in sweat n dreads
never weshed us bastard nets
in us little flat in Ferry
Dya remember when you smoked that salvia?
I did a cosmic lightshow on t'wall for ya

danced like a jewel box ballerina
on t'laminate effect linoleum
dint a?
I decorated t'flat wi rugs n books
we ad sod all but we ad enough
back then there w onny two of us
in us little flat in Ferry

MAKEOVER

You were fifteen and speeding
that night you gave me
a makeover

Your fingers smelt like nicotine
felt beautiful on
my face

firmly smudged foundation
removing all trace
of child

Wild cats eyes
all pupils
you smiled
approval
we looked
like twins

And I felt ten feet tall that night
bedazzled and bewitched
by my own
black eyes
I felt beautiful
for the first time

And now I want to do the same
for you

breathe love back
into the darkest parts of you
til your skin 's pink
and your breath's fresh
I can be
your reflection
at its best

Are you in? Are you in?
An are you still in there?
I'm struggling to see past
your mottled skin and matted hair
but there are glances , An
daft laughs
in my car
while I drive you to rehab

Flashing chances
of wit and spark
a distant sparkler
in the dark
there are fleks
of hope and
kindness in your heart
I can feel it

You take off your necklace
and put it on me

and in that moment
I know you're sorry

Black memories
fade to pink roses
Identical eyes
identical voices
take my tongue
and let it make your choices

Those ones you taught me
about fighting hard
and breaking free
your words An
I give them back

Use them like cement lass
and fill the cracks
remove
all trace of pain

IT'S ALRATE

it's alrate being a Knottla lass
it int that bad being skint n that
it's t'other stuff you can't talk abart
like your brother gettin stabbed
n your bike gettin nicked
n your cousin gettin spiked
n his head gettin bicced
n your best mate's nanna
gettin robbed in t'Spar
n Tommo selling gear
through t'window of his car
n Rielly chuckin rockets at
a lame Alsatian
n doin owwer t'bob shop
n t'cafe in t'bus station
n pulling art a needle
n gettin sent down
you can't escape the chaos
cause they'll glass you up
up town
n they're scrappin
artside Kiko's
n pukin up in cabs
dobbo's battered twokko

cos he called his lass
a slag n they're
pissed up on cheap cider
gettin a bit lippy

callin you a bitch
a freak a slag a cunt
a hippy
proper griefing you art
n spittin in yer hair
n you wonder why your parents
made you have to grow up there
n it never feels safe
n it int a fuckin joke
n the onny thing you've got
is lookin forward to some smoke
n rollin up a reefer
in your mate's dad's flat
cos it helps transcend the misery
n av a laugh
Your sister knows a dealer
she puts you both intouch
but you're onny just thirteen
you dunt know her all that much
you know she's called Scotch Barbara
she lives up by t'shop square
but you ant got her address
n they all look same up there
n it int an easy mission
n you wanna send your sister
but she's busy with the nipper
n you're gaggin for a bifter
so you fasten up your coat
you keep your head down

you hope your mam dunt see you
in that part of town
n you're dawdling around
at the end of someone's drive
the bulldog wants to kill you
rape you
eat you up alive
You daren't ask for Scotch Barbara
cos it really dunt sound raight
n someone's started kickin off
n askin for a faight
n you wanna go home
but you've come this far
n you can't leave empty handed
unless it's soapbar
n even then you'll probly tek it
cos it's better than nowt
even though it's full of plastic
n it's well harsh on your throat
n you skulk abart a bit
n you remember what she said
it's that one that's got
a trolley and a mattress
in the hedge
there's this woman
up in t'window
you're sure she's smokin dope
n you spot a dirty bed sheet
n you feel a twinge of hope

n she's a bit
like you remember
but you're not completely sure
so you loiter in the garden
til she opens up the door
n then you dunt know what to say to her
incase somebody hears
so you make this
tokin sign
like you've been scorin pot
for years
she nods her head
she gets it
she lets you go inside
she slices you a ten spot
you can't wait to get fried
She warms it up on t'fire
n t'baby's down on t'floor
n you feel all weird n guilty
that you're onny there to score
n the baby looks all dirty
n you dunt know what to say
so you fiddle wi your doccers
until it's time to pay
she wraps it in some clingfilm
you stash it in your coat
but she says you've gotta stay
n skin one up
n av a toke

n it feels rate uncomfy
it's not where you wanna be
cos you wanna go watch Neighbours
n your mam's made your tea
you've got nowt you can talk abart
she's scary n she's old
but it must be
toker's etiquette
to share one for the road
n you dunt wanna look stupid
or act like you're a nipper
so you knock a joint together
n poke it wi a clipper
n pass it to Scotch Barbara
when you can't smoke any more
chuck a fuckin whitie
av to lay down on the floor
Your mam's gunna kill you
it's startin to get dark
you're in Scotch Barbara's livin room
instead of at the park
the toilet's got no door on
there's nippers on the landin
what's that sticky yellow stuff
you've put your fuckin hand in?
N the young uns are all talkin
n askin you your name
n you're feeling cold n hot n sick
n scared n full of shame

n after twenny minutes
you mek it down the stairs
n Barbara looks indifferent
n you know nobody cares
n even though you've puked
n it's grotty weird n bleak
you know that you'll be back again
for more soapbar
next week

ALL HAIL THE ALBION FALLEN

All hail the Albion Fallen
losers, lovers, nymphs and thugs
tragic romantics
the Albion Fallen
indebted infected injected
in love

Spare a thought for the hearts of the Albion Fallen
beaten and broken and battered and bled
shed a tear for the fears of the Albion Fallen
dreaming of freedom
and waking up dead

take what you want from the Albion Fallen
take what you can
and fill in the cracks

take a leaf from the book
of the Albion fallen
get out while you can
and never look back

NIGHTS ARE FOR BREATHING

leaving t'day behind dreaming up plans reading abart gypsy
caravans and bicarbonate of soda
for checking your phone
like a pulse
Finding thoughtless awareness in t'teachings o' Tao mixing
vegan mao wi chickpeas
eating avocados
wi art all t'brown bits, please
n when t'writin dries up n your cup's empty
n words dunt wanna lek anymore
you could allers watch Come Dine wi Me
or Dunt Tell t'Bride
sometimes you've just gotta swallow your pride and embrace it
face it love
you're not a proper poet
just a trash TV addict
put the lid back on your pen
'cause you've ad it
Nights are for loving
praying
saying all t'stuff you wanna say
but dunt get t'chance
in t'thick o' t'day
imagining a better way
tomorrow

And in darkness
we're nowt but stars
and there's a stillness

that will either
tear you apart
or heal you
and I hear you
'cause it int allers easy
tryin to strike
a perfect balance
Be a matriarchal leader
democratic teacher
mother
and friend
and you've gotta forgive yoursen
when they drive you round t'bend
and you lose it
Ah, those nights wi happy hearts
are ace
when your kids fall asleep
wi a smile on their face
and the books on your head
are perfectly balanced

BREATHLESS AND PINK

at midnight the clock sprang forrad to Easter
twenty nine tinfoil eggs popped up surreptitiously
in shoes and drawers
landed softly on beds of angel hair
sat there sparkling
in your little tin buckets

You ate all of them for breakfast
except that one we couldn't find
I drove us to Co op
in brown sunglasses and furry coat
you said I looked like Gansta Mummy
it was one of them rides
where everything was funny and daft

We packed up a big bag of snap
and met dad at his land
you chose strawberries
and poppadums
and Mars Bar milkshakes

The sun shone high for our picnic
brought us to the
garden centre carpark
We walked along the turfed path
to the fields, til grey clouds
rolled owwer and exploded
spat fat wild hailstones

forced us pink cheeked and soggy
back to my car

We sat with the blowers on
eating crisps and drying out
and laughing about
how it always happens to us

We waited a bit
steamed up
to see if the storm would pass
and then drove back to ours
we enough stuff for me
to look after
all four of us

And then that egg that went astray
turned up later on in t'day
caught my eye
as it sparkled in t'felt tips
you held it carefully
in your tiny fingers
like a pearl
and then scoffed it

The sky filled our cottage
with sunlight and rainbows
as you scooted round the pub carpark
in your wellies

made your kite soar high in t'wind
you came in all breathless and pink
I made cups of tea
and thanked the universe
for my family

US FROM KNOTTLA

It's alrate being a knottla lass
catching t'bus to Pont or Cas
gobbing off n acting daft
am proud to be from Knottla

Grafting dads n barmy armies
swarms o' girls all dragging barbies
buttons missing from their cardies
lekkin art in Knottla

Boiled eggs n solidiers on a soft brown rug
mi mam supping her Horlicks from a Kellogs Cornflakes mug
mi Aunty Cath n Aunty Pam
hands on t'hips in 80s glam
stiletto heeled n pushing prams
proud as punch in Knottla

Shoulder pads n denim fellas
eyeshadder all shades o yeller
reading Bella supping Stella
sexy birds in Knottla

Broomhill Grove where Sandy's howlin
cross armed kids are brown n scowling
fowling footies tattooed dads are back from t'pit
and mams are sad
supposed to feed an army wi a tatie n some beans
keep their carpets hoovered n their nippers' faces clean

operate a twin tub n a sodding soda stream
they're hardcore mams in Knottla

Can mek a cracking pot o tea
Yorkshire puddings six bi three
av teld thi fatha nar am tellin thee
you dunt mess wi mams from Knottla

We've had a lot of shit up North
survival's in us blood of course
you waint find a stronger
prouder force
than us what come from Knottla

HOT PLASTIC MOON

it's all t'time these days a can't think straight need a break a fag
to lose some weight

it's all t'time these days and it dint usesda be all t'time not
much not much a bit a bit

a bit of a kick off now and again a bit of a hole-punch now
andagain when t'doorbell dringged or t'kettle shot hot clouds
from t'spout

first thing on a morning or last thing at night when you cunt
find your keys your cards your fags your trousers for work

when your mam rang in secret and went "aw he's had ard time
please understand he's had a tough ride just try to be loving
and loyal like me be busy making lists n cooking his tea and
popping to t'shop for Pepporami hots n bog roll n bin bags n
kitchen cloths be busy be thin just be good to him and you
waint even flinch when he bruises your skin cos you'll know
ahhh you'll know that he loves you too much to be yourself
loves you too much to watch you laughing wi somebody else"

but when it's all t'time it int easy to do it and when it's today I
waint ever get through it and there's nowhere to go when t'days
so late no change for a bus no credit no mates no sugar in
t'bowl to sweeten the blow and the kettle's on the lino

a hot plastic moon.

I WORE HOPE

I made my dress from all my lovers
a hot patchwork frock
stitching brother to brother
big belt hands wrapped tight around my waist
and warm mouths whispered in my ear
soft as lace
and I wore lust all day
and I wore lust all day

I made my dress from leaves and flowers
walked barefoot through concrete towers
threw down my hood
embraced the rain
and I wore hope all day
and I wore hope all day

I made my dress from all my sisters
stitched so long that I got blisters
pulled silver threads from moon to wombs
and I wore strength all day
and I wore strength all day

DARES NOT TO DREAM

Shit sticks in corners of forgotten towns
where mams shoot smack in dressing gowns
and old women
weathered as wellies
sit by themselves
sup pints
at eleven
no coffee mornings
for these
old lasses
no OAP yoga classes
they've come here to forget
they've come to put
their minds at rest
and what a fucking dreadful mess
what a fucking mess
They are strong
as Yorkshire tea
wear sovereigns like
Indian feathers
they are
chiselled from
the rocks of Leeds
this is where they live
and breathe
this is where
they cannot sleep
this is where they weep

at night
this is where they weep
And her head hurts
just there
 chicken hand
on silver hair
when she remembers
Blows smoke rings
up to heaven
wipes froth
on a buttoned sleeve
dares not to dream